PIANO/VOCAL SELECTIONS

DAVID JOHNSON and JESSE SINGER for ACT 4 ENTERTAINMENT JEFFREY RICHARDS WILL TRICE

GREENLEAF PRODUCTIONS REBECCA GOLD JOHN FROST TREVOR FETTER JOANNA CARSON
GORDON MELI PARTNERS CLIP SERVICE /A.C. ORANGE INTERNATIONAL NORA ARIFFIN JAM THEATRICALS ALMEIDA THEATRE
CENTER THEATRE GROUP PAULA & STEPHEN REYNOLDS J. TODD HARRIS
and THE SHUBERT ORGANIZATION
in cooperation with EDWARD R. PRESSMAN

Present

BENJAMIN WALKER

in

THE ALMEIDA AND HEADLONG PRODUCTION OF

AMERICAN PSYCHO
THE MUSICAL

Book by
ROBERTO AGUIRRE-SACASA

Music & Lyrics by
DUNCAN SHEIK

based on the Novel by BRET EASTON ELLIS

Also Starring
HELÉNE YORKE

JENNIFER DAMIANO DREW MOERLEIN

KRYSTINA ALABADO DAVE THOMAS BROWN JORDAN DEAN ANNA EILINSFELD JASON HITE
ERICKA HUNTER HOLLY JAMES KEITH RANDOLPH SMITH THEO STOCKMAN ALEX MICHAEL STOLL MORGAN WEED
BRANDON KALM SYDNEY MORTON ANTHONY SAGARIA NEKA ZANG

and
ALICE RIPLEY

Casting	Music Coordinator	Associate Director	Associate Choreographer	Company Manager	Production Stage Manager
TELSEY + CO	JOHN MILLER	WHITNEY MOSERY	REBECCA HOWELL	DANIEL HOYOS	ARTHUR GAFFIN
CRAIG BURNS, CSA					

Technical Supervisor	Press Representative	Marketing	Digital Marketing	Advertising	Executive Producer
HUDSON THEATRICAL ASSOCIATES	JEFFREY RICHARDS ASSOCIATES	TYPE A MARKETING	SITUATION INTERACTIVE	AKA	FORESIGHT THEATRICAL ALLAN WILLIAMS

Associate Producers
CARLOS ARANA JIMMY & SARA HENDRICKS BATCHELLER CTM PRODUCTIONS STELLA LA RUE
LUCY LEE JAMIE DEROY/TERRY SCHNUCK NATE BOLOTIN JAMES FORBES SHEEHAN

Orchestrator	Music Supervisor & Vocal Arranger	Music Director	Hair, Wigs & Make-up
DUNCAN SHEIK	DAVID SHRUBSOLE	JASON HART	CAMPBELL YOUNG ASSOCIATES

Scenic Design	Costume Design	Lighting Design	Sound Design	Video Design
ES DEVLIN	KATRINA LINDSAY	JUSTIN TOWNSEND	DAN MOSES SCHREIER	FINN ROSS

Choreography by
LYNNE PAGE

Directed by
RUPERT GOOLD

The Producers wish to express their appreciation to Theatre Development Fund for its support of this production.

ISBN 978-1-4950-6942-0

Cover art courtesy of AKA

HAL•LEONARD
CORPORATION
7777 W. BLUEMOUND RD. P.O. BOX 13819 MILWAUKEE, WI 53213

Visit Hal Leonard Online at
www.halleonard.com

4 CARDS

11 YOU ARE WHAT YOU WEAR

18 KILLING TIME

26 IN THE AIR TONIGHT

33 IF WE GET MARRIED

39 NOT A COMMON MAN

46 MISTLETOE ALERT

55 NICE THOUGHT

61 AT THE END OF AN ISLAND

68 I AM BACK

74 A GIRL BEFORE

80 THIS IS NOT AN EXIT

88 SELLING OUT (FISCHER KING REMIX)

97 EVERYBODY WANTS TO RULE THE WORLD

103 KILLING TIME 2.0

CARDS

Words and Music by
DUNCAN SHEIK

YOU ARE WHAT YOU WEAR

Words and Music by
DUNCAN SHEIK

Dance Beat

EVELYN:

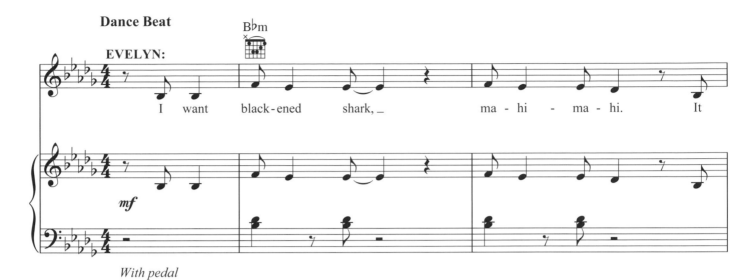

I want black-ened shark, __ ma-hi - ma-hi. It

COURTNEY:

works so well __ with I-saac Miz-ra - hi. I'll have so-da, and

EVELYN:

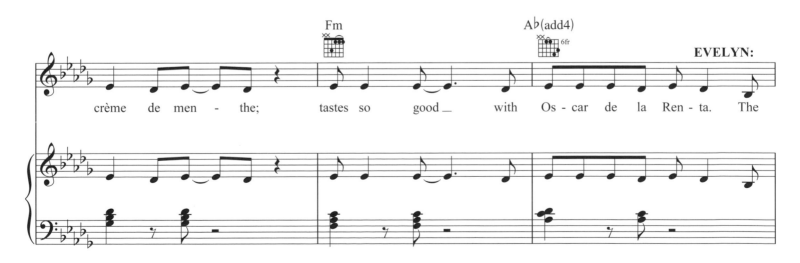

crème de men - the; tastes so good __ with Os-car de la Ren - ta. The

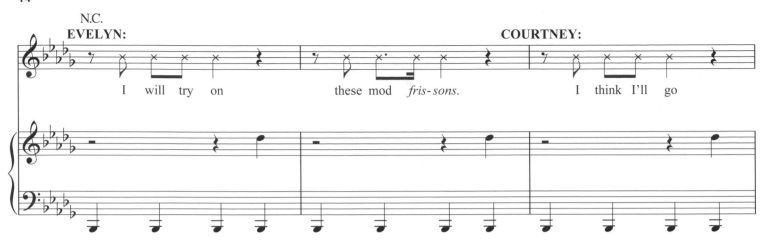

KILLING TIME

Words and Music by
DUNCAN SHEIK

Moderately fast Synth-Pop (half-time feel)

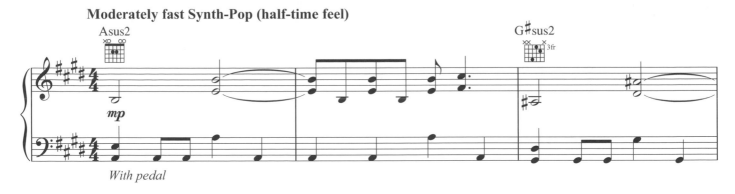

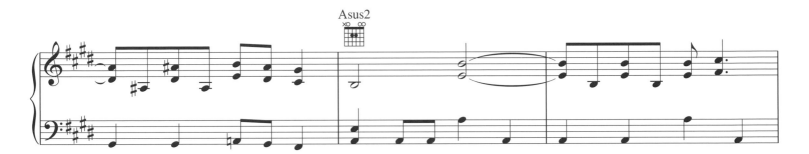

VOICE 1:

This can't go

on for-ev-er.   There's some-thing wrong.

VOICE 1:

fin - ish ___ line. ___ 'Cause

when you've made it, what will you find?

VOICE 2: 'Cause when you've ___ made ___ it, what

Heav-en's just a state of ___ mind. ___

will you ___ find? ___ It's my state of ___ mind. ___

BOTH:

You are not mov - ing moun - tains,

or chang - ing lives. _____ You're just

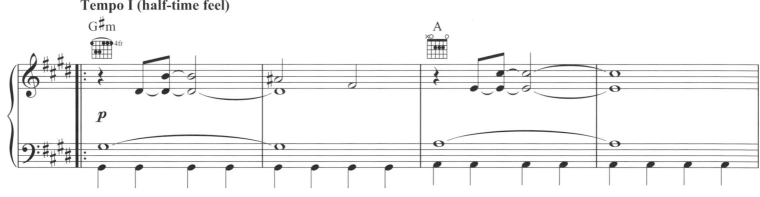

kill - ing while you're kill - ing ___ time. _____

Tempo I (half-time feel)

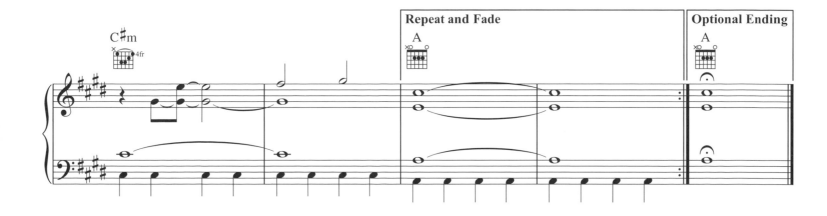

IN THE AIR TONIGHT

Words and Music by
PHIL COLLINS

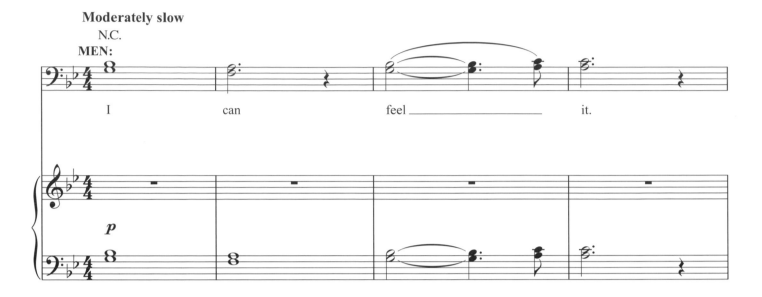

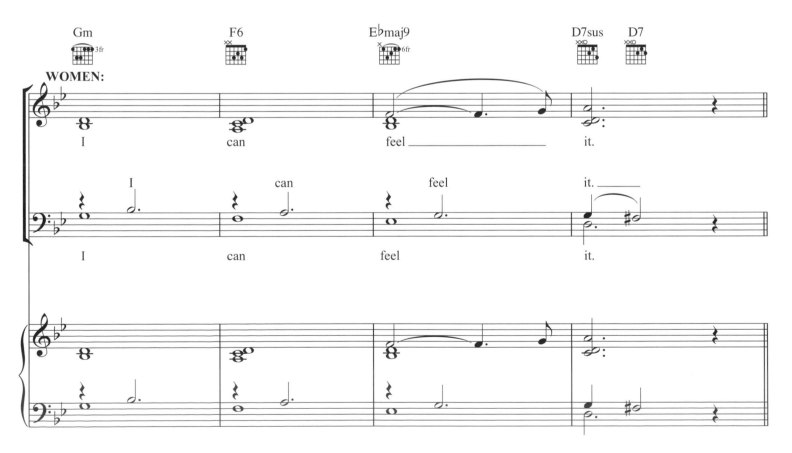

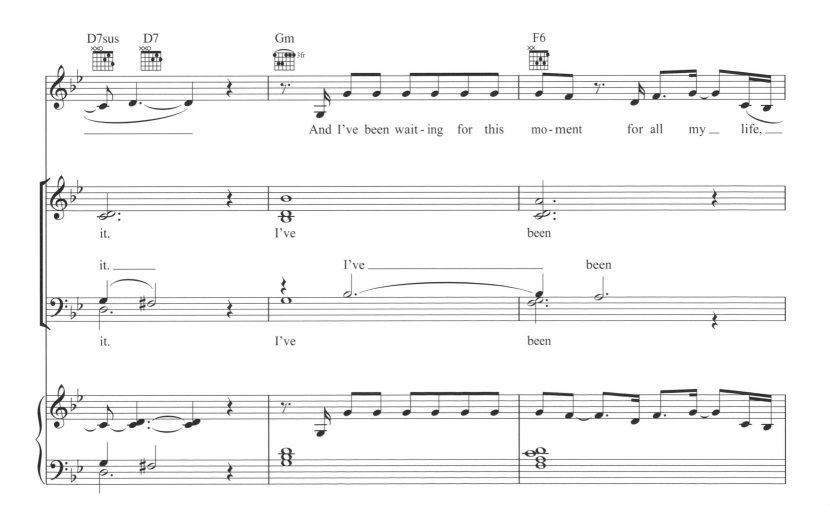

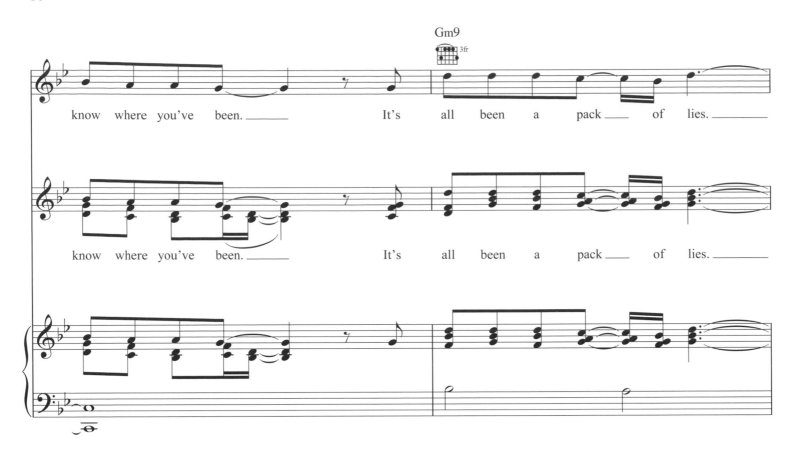

know where you've been. _____ It's all been a pack ____ of lies. _____

know where you've been. _____ It's all been a pack ____ of lies. _____

_____ And I can feel it com - in' in the air,

_____ And I can feel it com - in' in the air to - night, _

And I can feel it,

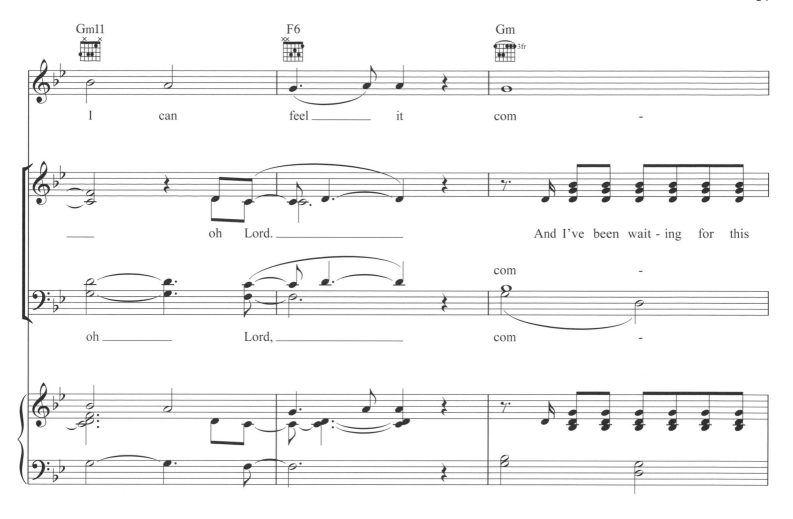

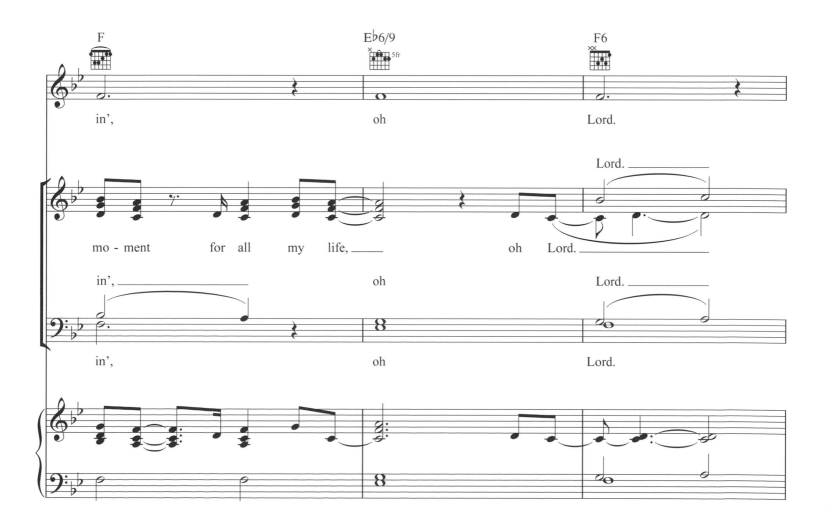

IF WE GET MARRIED

Words and Music by
DUNCAN SHEIK

NOT A COMMON MAN

Words and Music by
DUNCAN SHEIK

MISTLETOE ALERT

Words and Music by
DUNCAN SHEIK

NICE THOUGHT

Words and Music by
DUNCAN SHEIK

JEAN:

beau - ti - ful __ blonde curls; __ I knew one day __ he'd rule __ the world. It's a

nice thought: Pat - rick as __ a lit - tle __ child, __

play - ing at the sea - side, __ his spir - it free, his laugh - ter wild. __ It's a

nice thought, to think that un - der - neath __

AT THE END OF AN ISLAND

Words and Music by
DUNCAN SHEIK

I AM BACK

Words and Music by
DUNCAN SHEIK

A GIRL BEFORE

Words and Music by
DUNCAN SHEIK

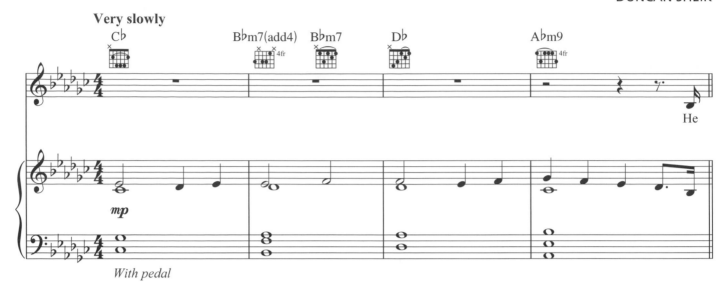

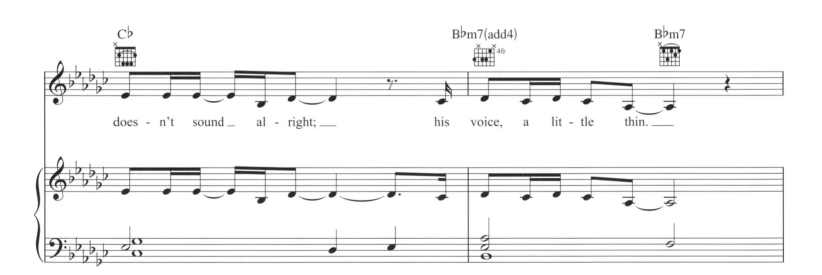

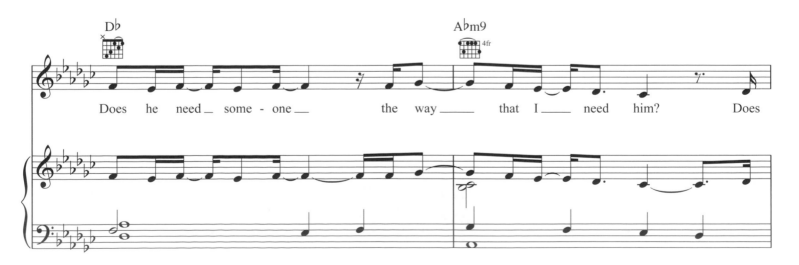

THIS IS NOT AN EXIT

Words and Music by
DUNCAN SHEIK

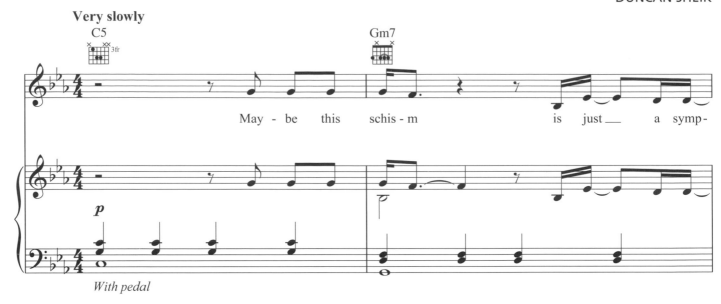

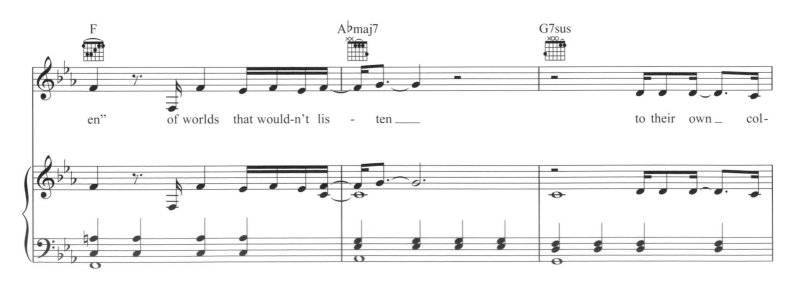

SELLING OUT
(Fischer King Remix)

Words and Music by
DUNCAN SHEIK

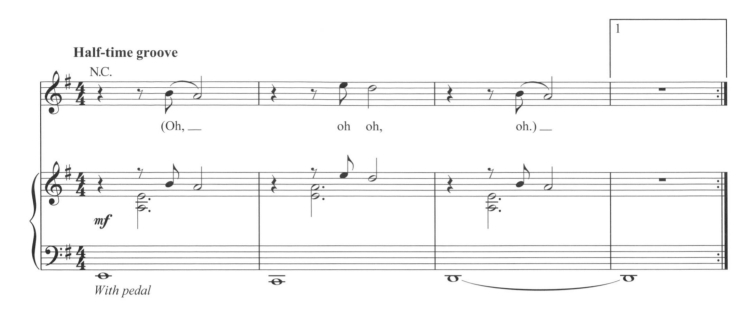

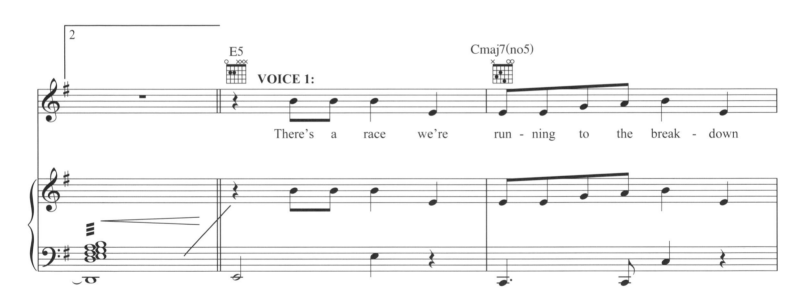

EVERYBODY WANTS TO RULE THE WORLD

Words and Music by IAN STANLEY,
ROLAND ORZABAL and CHRISTOPHER HUGHES

KILLING TIME 2.0

Words and Music by
DUNCAN SHEIK